COACHING THE TEAM PLAYER

DISCARD

by

Bobby Howe

WORLD of SOCCER

Vancouver

First published January 6th, 1992 by WORLD OF SOCCER
5880 Falcon Road, West Vancouver, B.C., CANADA, V7W 1S3

Tel: (604) 921-8963 Fax: (604) 921-8964

CREDITS:
Editor: Geoff Wellens
Illustrator: Martin Nichols
Copy Processing: Sharleen King
Graphics & Design: Lionheart Graphics

Printed in Canada by Hemlock Printers Ltd.

Canadian Cataloguing in Publication Data
Howe, Bobby.
Coaching the team player
ISBN 0-920417–11–6
1. Soccer—Coaching I. Title.
GV943.8.H69 1991   796.334'07'7   C92–091085–8

THE COACHING SERIES:

Coaching 6, 7 and 8 Year Olds

Coaching 9, 10 and 11 Year Olds

Coaching the Team

Coaching the Team Player

Coaching the Goalkeeper

OTHER WORLD OF SOCCER PUBLICATIONS:

Teaching Offside

Soccer is Fun — A Workbook for 6, 7 & 8 Year Olds

Micro Soccer - Rules and Regulations

Coaching to Win

From 3 vs 3 to 11 vs 11

ACKNOWLEDGEMENTS

West Ham United Football Club
AFC Bournemouth
Plymouth Argyle Football Club
Seattle Sounders

DEDICATION

To my Mom and Dad for their encouragement and inspiration and to my sister, Julie, for suffering the dinner table "Chalk Talks."

TABLE OF CONTENTS

INTRODUCTION

During the decade of the 1970s the Dutch National Team produced a style of soccer which was both innovative and exciting.

The style, later titled "Total Soccer," was created because of the multi-faceted talents of the players. Within the system of play, players were allowed to express themselves; they interchanged roles and rotated responsibilities but the balance and shape of the team remained intact.

The Dutch coach, Rinus Michels, had a wealth of talent from which to select and build a system and operated in a style to accommodate those talents. While youth coaches are not able to work with players of the same quality, the principles of building a team are the same; coaches must recognize the strengths and weaknesses of their players and use those players for the most part in areas of the field that will highlight their strengths and reduce the weaknesses.

In this manual I have used labels (names of positions) for functions in different areas of the field e.g. sweeper, center-back, central midfielder, center-forward, etc. I have also described some of the qualities required to play in those positions. As soccer is a team game, there is an overlapping of roles and responsibilities. In some cases qualities required to play one position may be suitable to play another, in other cases the qualities may be quite different. However, it must be understood by players that when they interchange positions, they must assume the responsibilities of the **new role**.

HIS & HERS

Throughout this manual the masculine gender has been used to describe players and coaches. This has been done for simplicity and clarity. *He/She* and *Him/Her* tend to interrupt the flow of information for the reader. I have spent a significant percentage of my coaching life teaching girls and working with girls teams; and my own daughter played high school soccer in Washington State. In my opinion there is no substantive difference in the coaching of boys and girls, and there is no "macho" intention within the book. The considerations and methods described in this manual will be just as appropriate to both genders.

PLAYER CODE

GK . . . . Goalkeeper	RMF . . . . Right Midfielder
SW . . . . Sweeper	CMF . . . . Central Midfielder
RFB . . . . Right Fullback	LMF . . . . Left Midfielder
CB . . . . .Center-Back	RW . . . . Right Winger
LFB . . . . Left Fullback	CF . . . . .Center-Forward
MF . . . . .Midfielder	LW . . . . .Left Winger
DMF . . . . Defensive Midfielder	S . . . . .Server

LEGEND

Path of Player	Path of Ball	Path of Player with Ball

HOW TO USE THE BOOK

This manual, like all our books in the *Coaching* series, is not a novel and, therefore, is not meant to be read from cover to cover in one sitting.

The **conditioned games**, the **functional practices** and the **attack vs defense** practices beginning on Page 45 provide the framework for **all positional play**. While the games described deal with specific functions, they may be adapted to emphasize other roles in the game.

I recommend that coaches use this book in the following manner:

- Identify the **positional problems** in the game.

- Select a game or games from the book which **highlight the positions**.

- Refer to the chapters on the **relevant positions** for related information.

- Refer to the chapter on the **coach** for additional information.

A recommended structure of a practice for players 12-16 years of age, "The Soccer Sandwich" is shown on Page 43.

Other information in this book will assist coaches in their observation of player performance and ability.

COMMUNICATION

Voltaire, the French philosopher, said, "If you would converse with me, first define your terms."

My first experience of coaching girls was in 1986 when I was appointed to work with the Washington State Olympic Development Program Under-14 girls' team. Hopefully, it was as much of a learning experience for them as it was for me!

I was the "expert" who, just three years earlier, had coached the Seattle Sounders in the professional North American Soccer League. Therefore, coaching young, inexperienced girls was "a piece of cake." Or so I thought! Unfortunately, I began to use the same terminology with the girls as I had with the pros—short, sharp commands which professional players understood through their experience. During one game I asked one of my players to "tuck in," meaning that I wanted her to apply a little more defensive cover. She looked at me and then at her attire and proceeded to tuck her shirt into her shorts!

The moral of the story is that communication is a two-way process and one of the keys to successful coaching. As coaches, we must ensure that what we are saying is the same thing being "received" by the players. The words we use must be totally understood.

QUALITIES OF A PLAYER

If asked what they are looking for when assessing soccer players, many experienced professional scouts would answer, "Can they play?" Indeed, old scouts would tell you that they could look at a game and "smell" a soccer player.

While there are many experienced coaches in this country who will understand this response, there are also many thousands of very interested coaches who require a much more detailed analysis. This chapter discusses the qualities a coach should observe when assessing individual player performance. You will note in following chapters that different roles in the game require different qualities; you will also see that there are different roles which require similar qualities.

In general, a player must know how to solve the problems that are presented by the game. On offense he must understand how to maintain possession of the ball, and on defense, he must have the desire to win the ball back immediately. Specifically, he must have knowledge of the game, skill, mental ability, impact and the fitness to play the game.

Knowledge of the Game

Positional Play

A player must have an understanding of the offensive and defensive functions of his position on the field of play.

Vision

Before he receives the ball he should be looking around to know what his options are so that when he is in possession he knows where to play the ball. An inexperienced player will think about his options to pass the ball only when the ball is at his feet. Quite often this is too late and could result in a loss of possession.

Awareness

At all times a player should know where he is on the field as his position relates to the position of the ball, his teammates and the opposition.

"Instinctive" Reaction

An experienced player will know how to react immediately in any given situation when under pressure himself or relieving pressure from a teammate. For example, on offense he will know how and where to run to create passing or shooting opportunities for himself or teammates. On defense, he will know how far and how fast to retreat or how quickly to challenge in order to avert danger. Thus, an experienced player appears to act almost by "instinct."

Adaptability

One of the many beauties of the game is that all players have the opportunity to be the quarterback. Whenever they are in possession of the ball they can affect the nature of the game. For this reason the player in possession must be able to adapt quickly to any given situation. Players off the ball, both on offense and defense, must adapt quickly to the constantly changing "pictures" in the game.

Inventiveness

There are many times in a game when a player has to use his own individual flair to create passing or shooting opportunities for himself or teammates. A player who has the ability to turn quickly, evade challenges easily, shoot when off balance and even perform his own "tricks" to create opportunities is an asset to a team.

Skill

Application of technique under pressure

There are many facets of the game which will cause a breakdown of technique. A good player will be able to maintain technical efficiency although he may be subjected to the pressures of the game. He will show composure under pressure of:

- The movement of the ball.

- The movement of his body with the ball.

- Opposition.

- A good player will also be able to perform skillfully under the pressure of fatigue. Concentration lapses and technique deteriorates when most players are tired.

Mental Ability

Confidence

In the make-up of a good player, physical ability goes hand in hand with mental ability. Not only must the player possess good skill, but also he must have the confidence to perform to his potential.

Mental Toughness

There are many things that happen in a game which may affect a player's confidence and concentration. For example, his team losing by more than one goal in the latter stages of the game; his team being totally dominated throughout the game; an individual breakdown in technique and constantly losing individual "battles" can all result in a loss of confidence and concentration. It is only the mentally tough player who will endeavor to perform to his utmost despite those odds.

Fitness

Endurance

Fitness is a very important component of the game. Not only must a player have the ability to play for the duration of the game, but also he must be able to recover (his fitness) while working in the game. Concentration lapses and skill levels tend to decline when a player is tired. The more soccer endurance the player has, the less chance he has of making an error through fatigue.

Speed

While speed of movement alone is most certainly an advantage to a soccer player, it is not vital. Speed of thought, however, is essential to success. Good perception and quick reaction can save much time. The following elements of speed combined are ideal.

Perception Speed is the time that elapses between the occurrence of a situation in a game and its recognition by a player.

Reaction Time is the time that elapses between the occurrence of the situation in a game and a player's initial physical reaction.

Speed of Movement is how fast a player is able to move over a distance of five to 15 yards.

Balance and Agility

A good player must have both static balance to resist challenge and dynamic balance (agility) so that he is in control of his body while moving either without the ball or performing a skill of the game.

Strength

There are many direct and incidental challenges in the game both on the ground and in the air. A player must have the strength to withstand those challenges.

Impact

A good player has the ability to affect greatly the nature of the game from his position on the field. Good goalkeepers, defenders, midfield players or forwards can all make an impact on the game from their respective roles in the team.

Summary

Quite naturally, not all players possess all the qualities stated above. Indeed, many successful professional and international soccer players do not have all those qualities. Therefore, when observing players for selection, a coach must take into consideration the standard of the game he is observing and the level of competition he is assessing. *One of the arts of coaching is combining the talents of players selected.*

COACHES HAVE NO EXCUSE

There is a popular story within the professional soccer "community" about two teams competing in a very important game. The score, with only ten minutes remaining, was 0-0. Suddenly a forward on one of the teams received a through pass but was clearly ten yards offside giving him an easy goal scoring opportunity. The player scored and the goal was allowed. On the way back to the center circle the referee was confronted by one of the opposing players: "That was no goal, he was way offside!" protested the player. "Oh, really?" replied the referee. "Read the newspaper tomorrow morning!"

This story provides an example of the same situation in the game viewed from entirely different perspectives: the player's and the referee's. There is another perspective, however, that we also should take into consideration—that of the coach.

The coach's perspective is entirely different from that of the player and the referee. No matter what his personality is like, *the coach cannot be impartial.* He will always be biased towards his own team.

Soccer coaches must not fall into the trap of copying coaches of baseball, football and basketball, where it is almost accepted to be highly critical of officials during the game. Also, there are no "time-outs" in soccer. In those traditional American sports the coaching staff can and do play a vital role in determining the result while the game is being played. Understandably, emotions tend to run high.

While emotions undoubtedly affect the soccer coach, he is under no real pressure during the game; he does not have to *run, sweat, or make split-second decisions as do the players and the referee.*

The nature of the game of soccer means that coaches can do very little to affect the outcome of the game while it is being played. As a result . . .

SOCCER IS A PLAYER'S GAME.

ARRANGEMENT OF PLAYERS

One of the most frequently asked questions from youth coaches at clinics relates to systems of play. Invariably they want to know the **best system**; the system that will win games for their team. Is 4-2-4 better than 4-3-3? What is the advantage, or vice versa, of 4-4-2 over 3-5-2, etc.? The answer, quite simply stated, is that systems by themselves do not win games.

Several factors must be taken into consideration before arranging the players to form a system:

- Players differ in their qualities and should be played in areas on the field where those qualities may be expressed, e.g. a player who has natural goalscoring ability but is a poor defender should be played as a forward. Not only will he be more comfortable in this position, but also, he will be a greater asset to his team.

- Most players will feel more comfortable playing on one side of the field than the other (a right-sided or left-sided player). Where possible those players should be used where they feel most comfortable.

- Successful teams have a fine balance of players who can score goals, players who can dribble, players who can distribute the ball and players who can defend.

- Even the most adventurous attacking team must not throw caution to the wind and have all the players rushing forward at the same time; a loss of possession would undoubtedly expose them to a counter attack.

- While teams must think positively on offense, they must attack in such a way that if they lose possession they have players well positioned to regain the ball.

- Even the most negative teams cannot afford to remain in their defensive third of the field for the entire game if they want to win.

- Teams on defense must have players in forward positions to play the ball to when they regain possession.

The shape and balance of the team changes as the game changes from offense to defense and from one side of the field to the other. Several examples are shown in the manual *Coaching the Team*. Please review the chapter, Deployment of Players.

Whatever number combinations are being deployed, certain common offensive and defensive **principles** must be observed.

The principles of play combined with technical development and understanding are foundations upon which the game is played.

One of the beauties of soccer is that all players on the field have the opportunity to play both offense and defense. When a team is in possession of the ball, the **whole team** is on the offense. When opponents are in possession of the ball, the **whole team** is on defense. The offense combines to maintain possession. The defense combines to gain possession.

Whatever the system being used, **ball possession** is the key to success.

Principles of Team Play

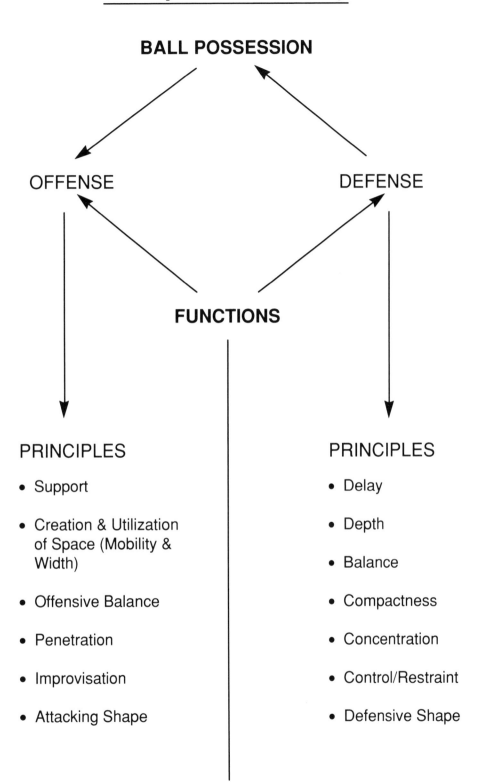

BALL POSSESSION

OFFENSE   DEFENSE

FUNCTIONS

PRINCIPLES

- Support

- Creation & Utilization of Space (Mobility & Width)

- Offensive Balance

- Penetration

- Improvisation

- Attacking Shape

PRINCIPLES

- Delay

- Depth

- Balance

- Compactness

- Concentration

- Control/Restraint

- Defensive Shape

INSTANT TRANSITION

ROLES OF THE TEAM PLAYER

OUTSIDE FULLBACK

Between 1930 and 1960 the position of outside **fullback** was not regarded as a glamorous role. Very often players selected to play this position were much slower and more cumbersome than their opponents (usually skillful, speedy wingers).

During the 1960s the role changed, faster players were used and much more offense was expected. The position became more attractive to play and the game more exciting to watch.

With the advent of the "modern game" in the last twenty years, where systems of play have changed dramatically, a fullback "type of player" is often used in wide midfield and, in many cases, has replaced the winger as the means of creating width and penetrating from wide positions on the field.

This chapter shows the importance of the fullback role and describes the qualities which make the position both effective and exciting.

Defensive Priorities

It must be understood by all players who operate at the back that their priority is to defend. Their offensive functions are a bonus.

Defending the strong side (ball side) of the field is much different to defending on the weak side.

In **Illustration 1**, the left fullback (**LFB**), who is playing on the strong side, is much closer to his opponent (**RW**) than the right fullback (**RFB**) is to his opponent (**LW**). This is because **LFB**'s opponent is much closer to the ball than the opponent of **RFB**.

Both fullbacks must ask the question, "If the ball were played to my opponent, could I get there at the same time?"

The advantages of **RFB** adopting the position shown rather than standing next to **LW**, as many young players do, are twofold:

- He can observe the movement of the ball and **LW** at the same time.

- He is easily able to deal with any balls played over the top of the defense (through passes) on his side of the field.

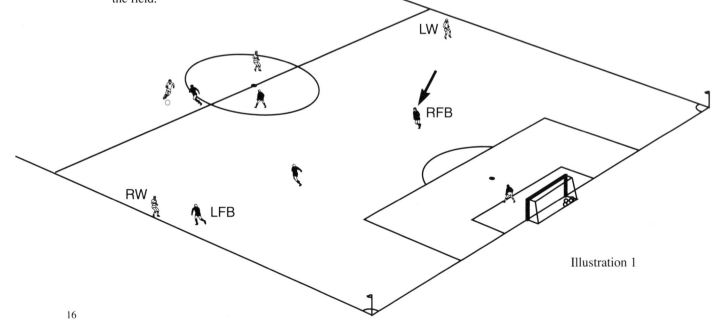

Illustration 1

Functions on Defense

Strong Side

In order of priority:

- Prevent opponent turning with the ball.

- Jockey opponent when the opponent is trying to dribble past.

- Tackle for the ball at the correct moment.

The fullback must be patient. His first responsibility is to delay the forward progress of the ball. In the defensive third of the field, his job is to prevent his opponent from crossing the ball. In both cases he should not **gamble** in his challenge for the ball; he should wait for the right moment and then **tackle aggressively**.

Weak Side

- Communication is very important. Excluding the goalkeeper, the weak-side fullback is very often the last line of defense. From his position he is able to see all the field of play. He is often the "eyes" for his teammates and must talk to them constantly.

- His position must **balance** the defense (**Illustration 1**). Not only must he be "in touch" with his opponent, but also, he must be in a position to prevent dangerous through passes.

Qualities on Defense

Strong Side

- Speed, quickness, agility and the ability to turn quickly are great assets for a fullback who is sometimes isolated in a wide position against a speedy, skillful opponent.

- Timing of tackles is important to success.

- While height is not a physical requirement of an outside fullback, the ability to jump to head the ball is a major advantage.

Weak Side

- Awareness of where he is on the field is important to the outside fullback role as his position constantly changes with the movement of the ball.

- The ball is like a magnet while in play; players are drawn to it subconsciously. The fullback must resist the temptation to "ball watch" while the play is on the other side of the field.

- Perception and reaction speed, recognizing a potential dangerous situation and dealing with it quickly, are vital to successful performance.

Illustration 2 shows the ball in a central position. The ball is away from **RW** and closer to **LW** than in **Illustration 1**. **LFB** can now afford to be further away from his opponent and **RFB** must move closer to his opponent.

Both fullbacks have similar functions:

- They can observe the movement of the ball and their opponents at the same time.

- They are able to reach their opponents at the same time as the ball.

- They are able to deal with through balls on their respective sides of the field.

Both fullbacks are helping to **balance** the defense.

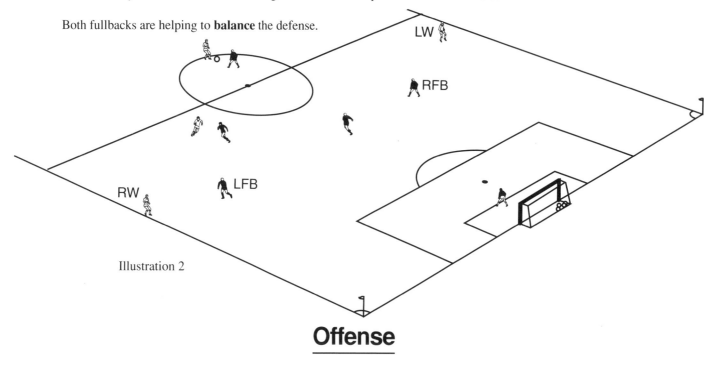

Illustration 2

Offense

Responsibilities

As stated earlier in this chapter, the defensive responsibilities of fullbacks are a priority. However, it is a tremendous asset to a team whose fullbacks support the play on offense and have the ability to function like forwards in the attacking third of the field.

Tactically, a team in possession of the ball tries to create a numerical advantage over its opponents anywhere on the field (e.g. 2 vs 1, 3 vs 2). A fullback is ideally suited to gain this advantage in wide positions especially in the attacking third of the field.

Offensive responsibilities and priorities change according to the area of the field in which the fullback finds himself.

Defensive Third of the Field

The offensive responsibility of the fullback starts the moment his team gains possession of the ball. For example, in his own penalty area where his goalkeeper has successfully made a save, he should break wide quickly outside the penalty area, to receive a possible pass from the goalkeeper. As he runs wide he should observe all the field of play and assess his options as to where he might play the ball should he receive it. His options are dictated by:

- The pressure of opponents

- Support of teammates

He must not gamble with his passes in this area of the field. A loss of possession could easily lead to an opposing goalscoring opportunity.

Midfield Third of the Field

As the midfield is the preparation area on offense, the fullback's main responsibility is to support the players in possession on his side of the field. While he may overlap or make forward runs for through passes from this area, his timing must be perfect. Before he makes a run in advance of the ball, his teammate in possession must have the ball comfortably under control and be ready to make the pass. A loss of possession in this area would result in the fullback being out of position and he would be forced to make a long, determined run to a safe defensive position.

Offensive Third of the Field

Strong Side

In the offensive third, the fullback on the ball side of the field functions exactly like a forward. Please review the chapter on "The Winger," Page 31.

In **Illustration 3**, **RFB** having assessed the space behind the defense, overlaps **RW**. **RW** plays a well-weighted, accurate pass into the path of **RFB**, as shown. The fullback crosses the ball.

Coaching Points:

- Timing of **RFB**'s run

- Timing of **RW**'s pass

- Pace of pass

- Space behind the defender

- Quality of cross

RFB may overlap only if **RW** is facing his opponents' goal.

If **RW** is facing his own goal with the ball, **RFB** should support and not attempt to overlap. The supporting position is shown in **Illustration 4**.

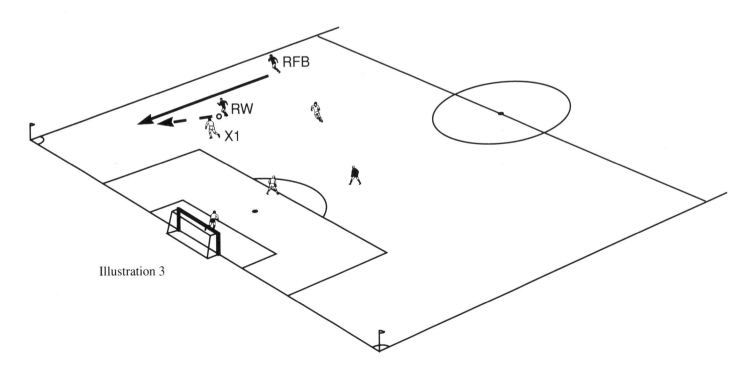

Illustration 3

Weak Side

In **Illustration 4**, **RW** is in possession of the ball in the offensive third of the field. **RFB** is in a supporting position and poised to overlap if necessary. Note the deep defensive position of **LFB**, who is helping to **balance** the offense.

The qualities required of the weak-side fullback in this position are the same as on defense.

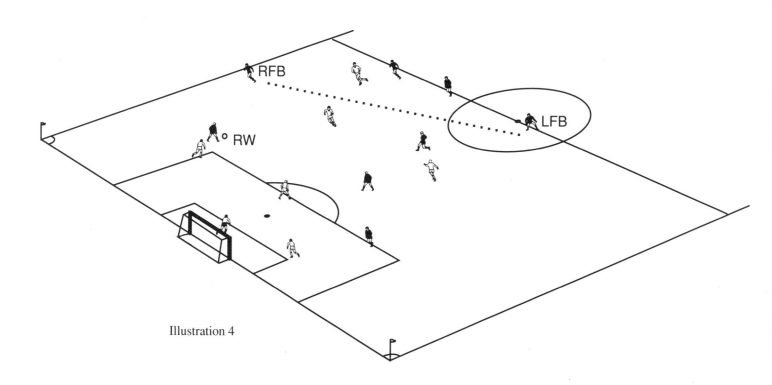

Illustration 4

While the strong-side fullback is encouraged to join in the offense, he may do this only with the knowledge that, should his team lose possession, there is safety in numbers at the back. In normal circumstances it would not be advised that **RFB** and **LFB** go forward at the same time.

SWEEPER

Most youth and senior teams in the world play with a free player behind their defense. This very important and exciting position is called the "Sweeper" in North America and the "Libero" in Europe.

While the priority for this "free man" is on defense, he may be equally effective on offense.

Defense — Midfield Area

When his team is on defense and the ball is in the midfield area, the role of the sweeper is to play free behind his teammates who are marking their opponents on a man-to-man basis. While he does not have a man-marking role, he does have the responsibility of support on the ball side of the field. Not only must he be in a position to assist a teammate who is challenging an opponent, but also, he must be in a position to deal with any potentially dangerous balls played over the top of his defense (through passes).

In **Illustration 5**, **X4** is in possession of the ball. The sweeper (**SW**) does not have the marking responsibilities of his other defenders. **LFB**, **CB** and **RFB** are marking **X1**, **X2** and **X3** respectively. However, **SW** is poised to assist any of his defenders should their opponents receive the ball. He is in a good position to deal with any balls that are played over the top of the defense.

Note the positions of **LFB** and **RFB**. While they are marking **X1** and **X3** on a man-to-man basis, they are not standing next to their opponents. Their positions, as shown, not only allow them to reach their opponents at the same time as the ball, they allow them to be first to any balls played over their heads and into the space behind them.

In dealing with through passes, the sweeper or his defenders must get to the ball quickly to allow themselves room and time in possession.

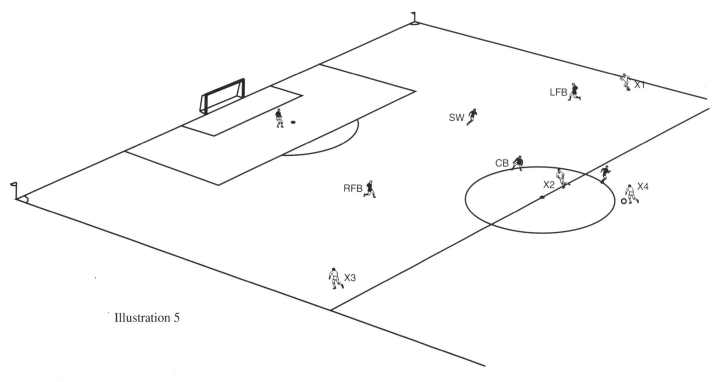

Illustration 5

Defense — Defensive Third

The sweeper's greatest responsibilities in the defensive third of the field are those of communication and organization. The nearer the ball is to his own goal, the less he is required to have a free role. Within the opponent's shooting range of his goal, he must communicate with his defenders as to who will pressure the opponent in possession of the ball. In many cases, it is the sweeper himself who will apply pressure either to make a tackle or, at least, to affect the quality of the shot.

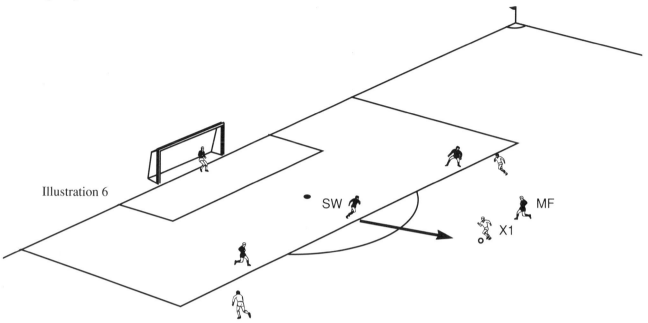

Illustration 6

In **Illustration 6**, **X1** has dribbled around **MF** and is moving into a dangerous shooting position. **SW** must move forward to apply pressure, as shown, to try to prevent a shot at goal.

While many sweepers are able to provide support when play is through the middle of the field, they are more reluctant to support when the play is wide.

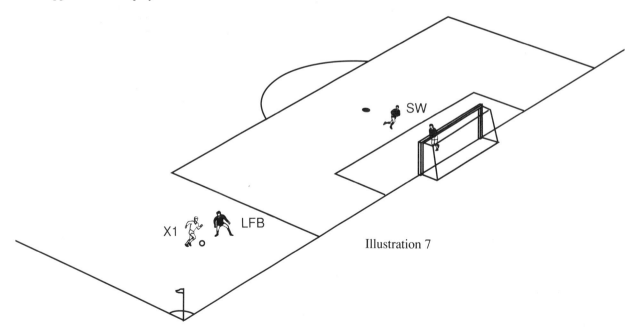

Illustration 7

In **Illustration 7**, the attacker, **X1**, is given a lot of room to take on his opponent, **LFB**. **SW** is waiting in the penalty area to deal with the potential cross.

In **Illustration 8**, **SW** has moved wide to help **LFB**, therefore giving the defensive team a much better chance to prevent the cross.

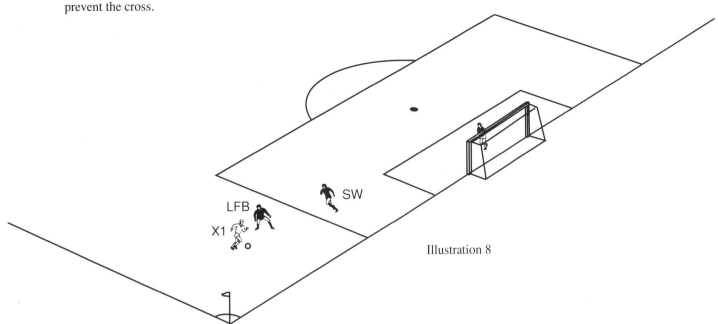

Illustration 8

It is always better to prevent the cross than to deal with a cross in the penalty area.

Offense

When experienced soccer people discuss the offensive qualities of a sweeper, they invariably talk about Franz Beckenbauer, the innovator of this role. Not only did Beckenbauer possess outstanding vision, awareness and passing ability, but also, the timing of his forward runs to support play were such that opponents found it extremely difficult to mark him or track him down. On many occasions, he was able to complete a move originating in his own third of the field by having a shot at goal in or around his opponents' penalty area.

The beauty of the position of sweeper on offense is that, with good timing and correct support, he is difficult to mark and is able to produce an element of surprise. However, it is important to understand that the forward movement of the sweeper at most times is in support of the play. Unless his timing is perfect, he should rarely make runs in advance of the ball. If play breaks down on offense, he should always be in a position to recover quickly to his free defensive role.

Summary

The qualities required to play this very important role are many and varied. On defense, the sweeper must have outstanding positional sense; he must know how to perceive danger and react quickly to deal with the problem. He must be able to organize and communicate. He is very often the last line of defense and from this position, he is able to "see what is on" and read the game for his teammates. He should have vision and awareness.

On offense, he should be an outstanding passer of the ball. Very often he is the initiator of an attack. He often has time in possession of the ball and should make the best use of the options that present themselves. The ability to support and time forward runs is also crucial to success.

The position of sweeper is exciting and important. The player selected for this role should have leadership qualities. Very often he is the captain of his team.

CENTER-BACK

The center-back or central defender or "stopper" as he is also known, is the pillar at the center of the defense. Like his fellow backs, his priority is to defend. One of his main functions is to combat the threat of the opposing team's center-forward.

Qualities on Defense

Main Qualities

The qualities required to play this position are very similar to those of the outside fullback:

- He must prevent his opponent turning with the ball.

- He must be patient.

- It is vital that he knows how and when to tackle for the ball and that he does not over commit. Timing is the key to success.

- Errors of judgement in a central position can be very costly. When attempting to intercept a pass before it reaches his opponent, he must be certain that he will reach the ball before the opponent. Poor judgement could result in being out-maneuvered and turned.

- At most times he operates in the center of the defense and is the axis about which the defense pivots. It is for this reason, at all times, he must be aware of where he is on the field as his position changes with the movement of the ball and the movement of his opponent.

- Communication with other defenders and his midfield players is also vital to successful performance.

Positional Play

When marking his opponent, the center-back should always try to take an "inside line" on his opponent. Not only should he be on his own goal side of the opponent, but also, where possible, on the ball side of his opponent.

Taking the "Inside Line"

Illustrations 9, 10 and 11 on the next page show the ball in a midfield area (midfielder, **X1**, is in possession) and three separate positions of the center-forward, **X2**.

Note the position of **CB** in each example; his position changes according to the position of his opponent.

- He is not standing immediately behind his man; his position gives him a clear view of the ball and he is poised to intercept the pass where possible.

- He is goal side (nearer to his own goal) of his opponent.

- He is "inside" the line of his opponent to the ball.

- In each example, should his opponent receive the pass from **X1**, he is making it difficult for the forward to turn towards the goal.

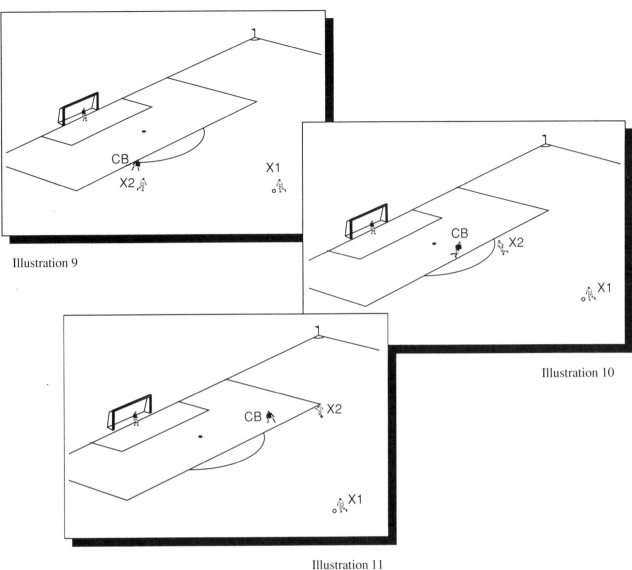

Illustration 9

Illustration 10

Illustration 11

Physical Qualities

It is an advantage for the center-back to have athletic ability or to be taller than the average player. Very often his opponent is skillful, possesses good shooting ability and is good in the air.

The center-back must combat those qualities, therefore:

- He should be good in the air.

- While speed of movement is most certainly an advantage, **perception, speed and reaction speed are vital to success**.

Good defenders perceive potential danger—bad defenders react to a crisis.

Qualities on Offense

The qualities required of a center-back on offense are similar to those of a sweeper in the previous chapter.

He is often a very dangerous "weapon" to use at offensive set plays in and around the opponent's penalty area. If he possesses good physical qualities, a team must make maximum use of this advantage.

MIDFIELDERS

The midfield area of play requires skills which are many and varied. The **midfielders** bear the major responsibility for forming attacking play either by dictating the pace or tempo of the game where the ball is played through midfield, or by supporting the forward players intelligently when the ball is played over midfield.

Whenever and however teammates or opponents move on the field, corresponding adjustment is demanded from the midfield player.

Whatever system is being used by a team, offensive and defensive balance in midfield is vital to success. The midfielders need to scheme creatively, to defend resolutely and to score goals. As most players do not possess all these qualities, successful teams will coordinate the skills of different types of players so that the midfield functions as a well-rounded unit.

The Defensive Midfield Player

The Windshield Wiper

In a team where one midfield player may be used as a second attacking spearhead operating just behind a forward or forwards, or in a team which uses two offensive-minded central midfielders, the midfield balance may be restored by using a defensive midfield player. The main priorities for this player are on defense; anything he does on offense should be regarded as a bonus to the team. He operates in a position just in front of the back players and, like his fellow defenders, he possesses good defensive qualities. In modern soccer he is sometimes called a "Front Screen" or "Windshield Wiper."

At times he may be asked to mark man-to-man an opposing midfield player who may be regarded as the main threat to his team. This role will take him to all areas of his own half of the field and to some areas of his opponent's half. In this case, balance in midfield must be restored by other players.

When he does not have a specific marking responsibility, the defensive midfielder will operate in a position just in front of his back players, as shown in **Illustration 12**. From this position he may look to intercept passes played to the feet of opposing forwards. He cannot allow any opponent free possession in an area just in front of his own defense; he must close that player down very quickly to put the opponent under pressure.

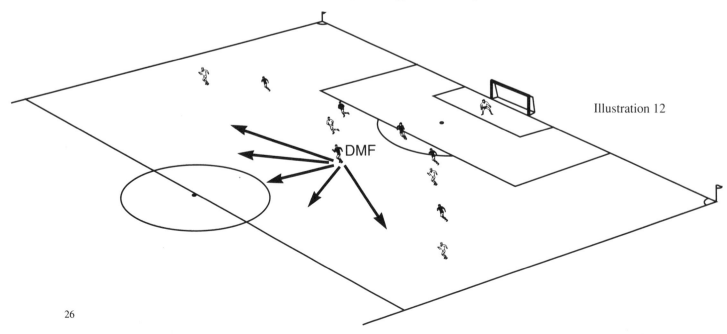

Illustration 12

Qualities of a Defensive Midfielder

- Should know how and when to pressurize an opponent in possession of the ball and make it difficult for that player to penetrate.

- He should always be under control so that he does not "sell himself" in the challenge.

- If an opponent is facing away from goal, he should not allow that player to turn with the ball.

- He should have good perception and reaction speed, and good awareness of his position as it relates to the ball and his opponents.

- He must be prepared to run with and stay goal side of an opponent who makes a run into the penalty area.

- He must be prepared to interchange positions with his defenders when they have moved forward on offense.

- Not only must he be a good communicator with his midfield players and back players, but also, he must be able to react quickly to instruction.

Offense

While his ability to win the ball for his team is his most important role on defense, it is also his primary function on offense. Winning the ball is the beginning of offense.

The forward movement should be, at most times, in support of the play and not in advance of the ball. On occasions, when he is able to make well-timed runs in advance of the ball, his position should be filled by another midfield player so that balance is maintained.

The Midfield Playmaker

Orchestration

If a soccer team were an orchestra, the midfield playmaker would most certainly be the conductor, dictating the pace and rhythm. While his responsibilities are always creative, his starting position or his defensive base will be dictated by the style and system used by his team. For example, in a 4-3-3 system, he would be effective as the central midfield player. In a 4-4-2 system he would operate in one of the two central midfield positions. In some cases both central midfielders operate as creative schemers. One or both midfield players in a 4-2-4 system may have the playmaking responsibilities and one or two of the three central midfielders in a 3-5-2 may act as the playmakers.

Irrespective of the system being used, offensive and defensive balance must always be maintained by using players with different qualities.

Responsibilities

As the link player, he must always be available to take over the ball to set-up an attack. When in possession he must know how and when to combine with other players extracting the maximum out of their strengths but being aware of their limitations. His attacking play is always thoughtful, knowing when and where to make short passes; when and how to penetrate opposing lines of defense by dribbling or using the wall pass; knowing when to use the long or short penetrating through pass to create goalscoring opportunities and knowing when and how to change the point of attack.

He must run with the ball intelligently and at a pace that he dictates based upon what he "sees" in the game. He must also take the responsibility of shooting when the opportunity is created for him or is created by himself.

When his team loses possession in midfield, his immediate responsibility is to delay the forward progress of the ball to allow teammates to retreat quickly to safe defensive positions. He must drop back on defense at the same rate as the opposing attack but ensuring that he is on his own goal side of the ball.

Finally, the moment his team has regained possession, he must make himself available to take over the ball again.

Qualities

- He is a leader on the field; he demands from himself and teammates.

- His functions demand that he plays through 360 degrees; he must have great awareness of where he is on the field and always know where to play the ball before he receives it.

- He must have excellent vision, seeing all the options available.

- Outstanding skill is vital to this role. Not only must he be able to see the options, but also, he must have the ability to play the ball to an option which, at that time, will have the most impact on the game.

- He must be athletic and possess outstanding endurance to fulfill the potential of the role, combining creative offense with responsible defense.

- He must be brave in his decision making and mentally tough; he is one of the players to be relied upon to drive his team on despite the odds.

The Outside Midfield Player

Balancing

The midfield is very often called the "engine room" of a team, an expression which denotes driving force or energy. A player operating in wide midfield positions must promote this energy by his willingness to join in the creative offense of the team and also track back on defense. He must think like a winger in the offensive third of the field and like an outside fullback in the defensive third. He must be able to provide width on offense when play is on his side of the field and both offensive and defensive balance when play is on the opposite side.

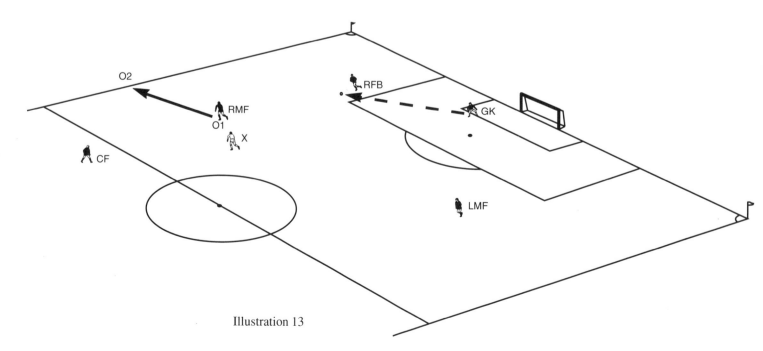

Illustration 13

Importance of Width

In **Illustration 13**, **RFB** is receiving a short pass from his goalkeeper. As the ball is played to **RFB**, **RMF** must pull wide to the touchline (from position **O1** to **O2**) to create more options for **RFB**. If he does not go to the wide position, he will not pose any problems for his opponent, **X**. In fact, in this position, **X** is doing two jobs; he is putting pressure on **RMF** and also, he is preventing a simple pass from **RFB** to **CF**. If **RMF** runs wide, he poses a problem for **X**. Should **X** run wide to mark **RMF** or should he stay to prevent a pass to **CF**? In either case he cannot prevent his opponents from keeping possession of the ball. At position **O1**, **RMF** has his back to play and would have limited options to pass the ball should he receive it. At position **O2** he is able to see all the field and, therefore, all the options.

Note the balanced position of **LMF**. He is in an ideal position to spring forward on offense and also ideally placed to lend a hand on defense should his team lose possession. If he were too wide he would not be "in touch" with play.

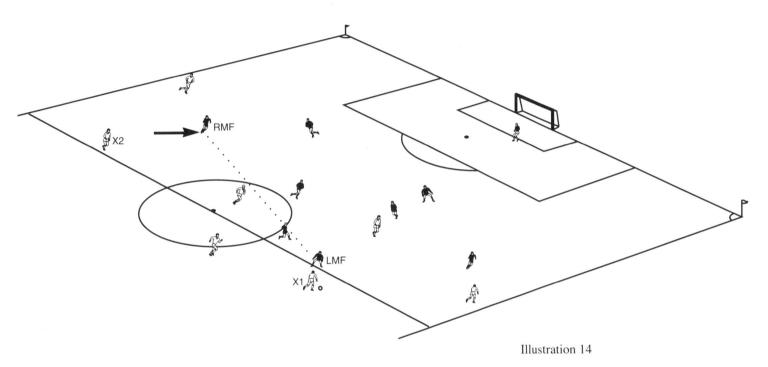

Illustration 14

Defensive Balance

In **Illustration 14**, **X1** is in possession of the ball. He is challenged by **LMF**. Note the defensive position of **RMF**. His diagonal position, as it relates to the ball, offers balance to his team. He is his own goal side of the ball and his immediate opponent, **X2**. From this area he is able to see both the ball and his opponent comfortably and he is in a position to perform two functions:

- To prevent a penetrating through pass on his side of the field.

- To challenge **X2** should that player receive a crossfield pass from **X1**.

Except on very rare occasions where he is allowing his opponent to run offside, he should never allow **X2** to be behind him when he is on defense.

He is also well placed to spring forward on offense should his team regain possession.

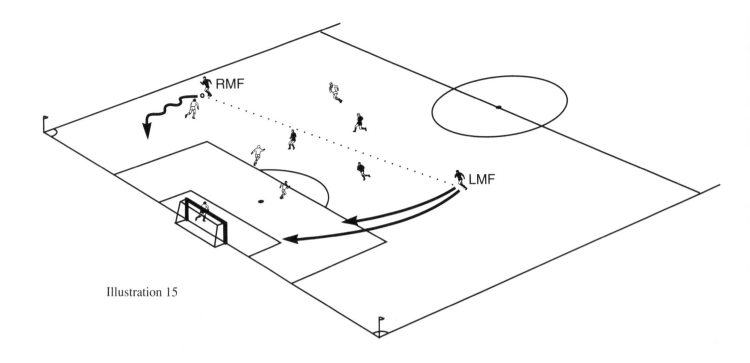

Illustration 15

Offensive Third of the Field

Illustration 15 shows **RMF** in possession of the ball taking his opponent on and crossing the ball. In this situation he functions like a winger.

Note the starting position of **LMF** compared to **RMF** (**LMF** is diagonally behind the ball). **LMF** has to assess the progress of the player with the ball and make forward runs accordingly. His runs will be dictated by two factors:

- His starting position

- His ability

The latter will determine whether he supports on the edge of the penalty area to deal with flick ons or half clearances or to run into the penalty area to challenge for the ball.

If he makes a run into the penalty area, balance on the edge of the penalty area must be restored by a central midfield player.

Qualities

On offense the outside midfielder operates like a winger and on defense he acts like a fullback.

In a 3-5-2 system, where the wide midfield player does not have an outside fullback operating behind him, the wide midfield player should be a fullback type of player rather than a forward type of player. He sometimes has to defend in 1 vs 1 situations and often has to track back to remain goal side of his opponent. A fullback is much better equipped to do this than a forward.

Strong running ability and endurance are very valuable assets to play this role. However, intelligent positional play, saving a great deal of unnecessary reactionary running, is the key to success.

WINGER

One of the most exciting aspects of the game of soccer is to see an outstanding **winger** in action and one of the most interesting duels in the game is the "cat and mouse" play of the winger and his immediate opponent, the outside fullback. In a game where both teams are operating in a 3-5-2 system, the duel is created by opposing wide midfield players.

The winger's starting position is on either touchline and it is how he operates in that area to create space for himself or teammates that will determine success for himself and, in many cases, for his team.

In most cases, wingers are used in a 4-2-4 system or a 4-3-3 system.

In the latter, there may be one winger and two strikers or two wingers and one striker.

Offensive Qualities

While size has not appeared to be a significant factor to successful wing play, there are several required qualities that are vital to success.

He must be quick off the mark with the ball and quick over the first ten yards to escape challenge.

Once he has made his angle to cross the ball, he must get the cross in immediately and not try to beat his opponent again. Delay or indecision in crossing the ball may destroy the runs of his forwards into the opponents' penalty area.

While the cross should be accurate, the winger should not try to pinpoint a teammate. He should recognize the opponents' danger areas (areas not easily reached by the goalkeeper) and try to play the ball into those areas.

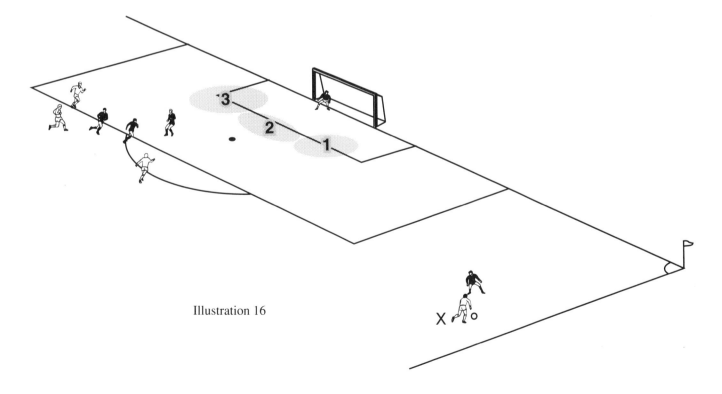

Illustration 16

In **Illustration 16**, **X** is the winger in possession of the ball. His three main target areas are shown. Area 1 is the near post zone (nearer to the ball), Area 2 is mid-goal, just outside the goal area and Area 3 represents far post zone. All three areas create indecision for the goalkeeper - should he come for the ball or should he stay on his goal line? The winger's responsibility is for the accuracy of the cross. Timing is the responsibility of the player receiving the cross.

- The winger must be a strong dribbler and clever at evading tackles.

- He must be both cunning and lethal and must never give up.

- On many occasions he will be felled by slide tackles. He must have the determination and bravery to continue, otherwise, he will be lost from the game.

- In the final third of the field, he must possess the ability to combine in the initiation of wall passes for penetration.

- He must also have the individual penetrating ability and courage to go outside his opponent to cross the ball or inside his opponent to finish with a shot at goal.

- When play is in the opposite side of the field, the winger must move forward at the same rate as the ball and, depending upon his strengths, either move into the penalty area to challenge for a cross or stay just outside the penalty area to redirect "flick ons" or over hit crosses.

Defensive Qualities

- On the strong side, he must stay goal side of his opposing defender to prevent that player from supporting or overlapping successfully.

- On the weak side, he must maintain defensive balance in the same way as a wide midfield player.
  See previous chapter.

Summary

Dribbling past an opponent with the ball is a difficult skill. In many cases, it provides a low percentage success rate. For this reason, many coaches have discouraged players from dribbling and have adopted tactics to exclude wingers.

- Players with outstanding dribbling ability should be encouraged.

- They should be shown the most effective areas to dribble.

- They should be shown how to combine with teammates; when to pass the ball and when to take an opponent on.

In an era when individual flair gives way to methodical buildup, it is refreshing and exciting to see a winger "in full flight."

CENTER-FORWARD

The **center-forward** or "striker" or "target man" has undoubtedly the "glory" role on the soccer field.

While a player can be taught the areas in which to challenge for the ball to obtain goalscoring opportunities and, while practice will improve timing in getting into those areas, the art of goalscoring is almost a natural gift. Players who have this "natural" ability should be played in areas of the field where they are going to get the maximum number of goalscoring opportunities. The position of center-forward is ideally suited.

Whatever system is being used, a team should always have a center-forward or two center-forwards who share the work load up front. This position is so important that when the center-forward(s) is not functioning well, the team will not function properly.

While the position of the center-forward provides many opportunities to score goals, it is a very difficult position to play because the player has to perform with his back to the opponents' goal for much of the game.

Offensive Functions — Ball in the Central Areas

The center-forward must always provide an option for teammates to play the ball forward to him. In order of priority he should make runs:

- To receive the ball **behind** the opposing defense **(Illustration 17)**.

- To receive balls to feet **in front** of the opposing defense **(Illustration 18)**.

In both cases timing of the run and control are keys to success.

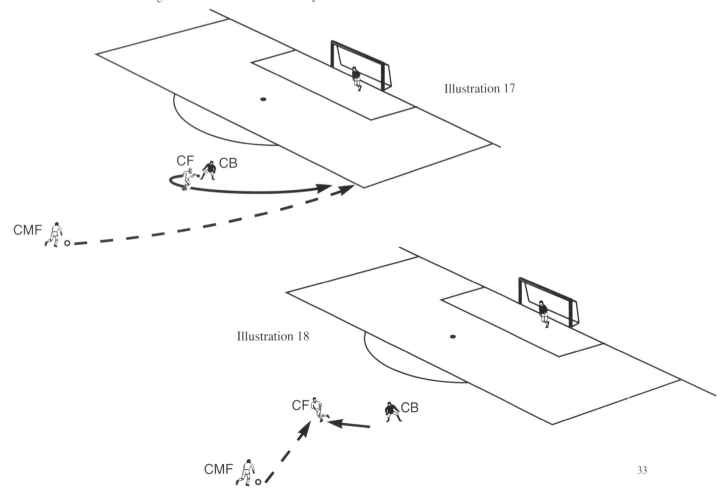

Illustration 17

Illustration 18

33

In **Illustration 17**, **CF** makes a run towards his teammate, **CMF**, as shown; the run is made to draw **CB** towards the ball and create space behind the defender. **CF** turns and accelerates into the space behind **CB**. This is a **diagonal** run rather than a straight run towards the goal because it:

- Creates more space for **CF** to receive the ball.

- Allows him to see the flight of the ball.

- Creates a bigger target area for **CMF** to play the ball.

In **Illustration 18**, **CF** makes a run to try to get behind **CB** and then checks to receive the ball in front of the defender. **CF** does not check in a straight line towards the player with the ball but at an angle, as shown. The line of his run:

- Allows him to receive the ball easier with his front foot.

- Allows him to see more of the field of play as he receives the ball.

- His position on the half-turn gives him an option to turn his opponent and take him on.

- Sets himself up to return the pass to **CMF** and quickly accelerate into the space behind **CB**.

Offensive Functions — Ball in Wide Areas

The primary target areas for players with the ball in wide positions are shown on Page 31, **Illustration 16**.

The responsibility of the center-forward is to **attack** those areas and to try to arrive **at the same time as the ball**.

- The quality of the cross is the responsibility of the wide player.

- The **timing of the run** is the sole responsibility of the receiver.

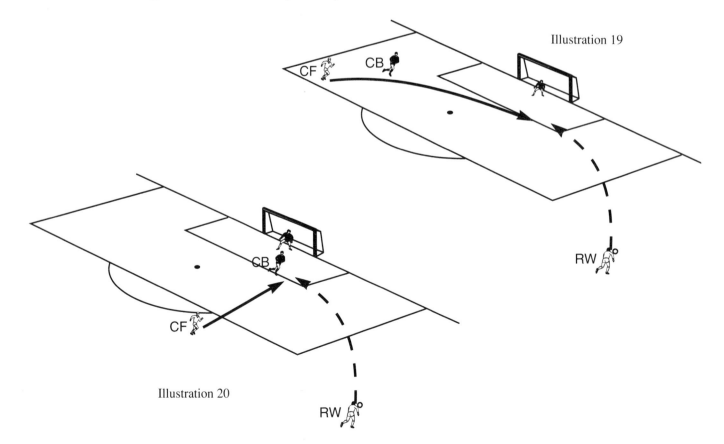

Illustration 19

Illustration 20

In **Illustrations 19** and **20**, **RW** is in possession of the ball outside the penalty area.

In both illustrations, **CF** times his run to arrive at the near post area at the same time as the ball. However, the run in **Illustration 19** presents a much better opportunity for him to score.

His run from behind the defender and towards the ball has two advantages:

- **CB** is not able to look at the ball and **CF** at the same time.

- **CF** is more able to judge the line of the cross.

Qualities on Offense

- He must work hard to "show" for the ball so that his teammates always have an option to play the ball forward to him.

- He must be unselfish in his running and very patient, knowing that in most of the runs he makes to offer himself as an option for a pass, he will not receive the ball.

- He must have outstanding control and shielding ability to hold the ball and maintain possession while waiting for support.

- While he should play the ball simply and efficiently in the midfield area, in the offensive third of the field he should have the ability to improvise to create goalscoring opportunities for himself or teammates.

- He should be both clinical and ruthless in his finishing in and around the opponents' penalty area. Surprise changes of speed, outstanding perception and quick reaction are vital to his success.

- He must be determined, assertive and explosive in front of goal, yet he must be cool under pressure.

- Outstanding heading skill is most certainly an advantage. Not only must he be able to challenge for high crosses, but also, he must be able to re-direct aerial passes to the feet or into the path of teammates.

- When a team is operating with dual center-forwards, both players must have timing and understanding. They must know how to create space for themselves and each other. For this reason they must practice constantly as a "team." It is said that all successful twin strikers "hunt in pairs."

Qualities on Defense

Much of the center-forward's work is on offense. Therefore, much of his energy should be directed towards the attack. However, when opponents are in possession "goal side" of the center-forward, he should work hard to delay the forward progress of the ball. He should also pursue his opponent if he loses possession to that player and fight to regain the ball.

GOALKEEPER

There are many experts of the game who believe that the position of **goalkeeper** is the most important on the field. While I believe that to be a matter for conjecture, it is certain that the goalkeeper requires ability which is much different to that of an outfield player. Within the penalty area he has the great advantage of being able to use the reach of his arms and to use his hands. No other player on the field is afforded this privilege.

It is important that a goalkeeper receives special attention in some practice sessions. Time spent alone with the goalkeeper(s) before, during or after a normal practice session will undoubtedly improve technical performance.

While techniques are very important, most young goalkeepers (12-18 years) have much more of a problem with their tactical understanding of the position. Indeed most mistakes occur because of **poor decision making**.

Therefore, most of the goalkeeper's practice should be with the rest of the team so that he has to make decisions, communicate with teammates and practice his techniques under the pressures of the game.

Goalkeepers should be used in all the conditioned games and functional practices described later in this book.

A Good Start

The starting position for the goalkeeper is vital to successful performance. His position is dictated by the position of the ball on the field. His position in many circumstances is also dictated by his size and/or his agility. When the goalkeeper has advanced off his line, he has to calculate the risk of a ball being played over his head. If he is constantly aware of his position as it relates to the ball and the goal line and if he knows, in an advanced position, he could get back to deal with a ball played above his head, and that he is creating a limited opportunity for a successful chip shot, that is **a good start**.

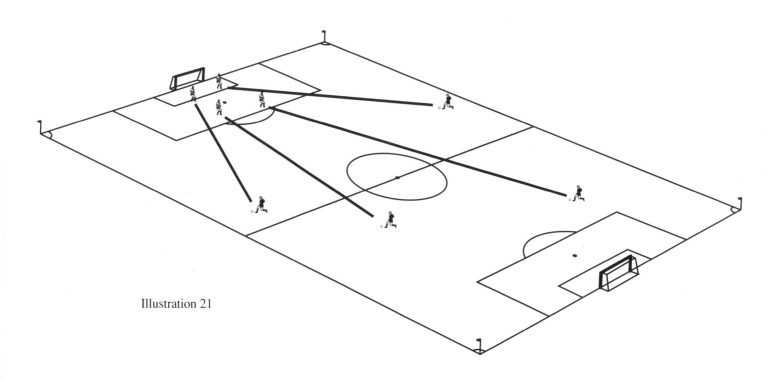

Illustration 21

Illustration 21 shows the further the ball is away from the goal line, the further the goalkeeper may advance off his line. Because of the size and agility factor, the advanced positions in the illustration are approximate. However, note that the goalkeeper is always on a line between the player in possession and the goal.

A successful goalkeeper is always on the move, constantly checking his position. Not only does this enable him to communicate and keep in close touch with his defenders, but also, it allows him to deal more successfully with through balls.

Although the position does not require any more concentration than that of an outfield player, it is the hardest position to maintain concentration because of long periods of inactivity. Constant movement helps concentration and it keeps the goalkeeper involved and alert.

The position of goalkeeper is the only mandatory position on the field.

While he does not always receive the accolades of the goal scorer, his performance can affect greatly the outcome of the game. If his performance is poor, he can lose matches on his own account. If his performance is good, he will give his teammates confidence and often inspire them to play above themselves.

The position of goalkeeper is special and different enough from field players to require different qualities. It is for this reason that Tony Waiters has written the book, *Coaching the Goalkeeper*. Before working with your goalkeeper(s) I recommend that you read the book which is also in our "Coaching" series.

OFFENSE AND DEFENSE

I have stated elsewhere in this book that all players on the field have the opportunity to play both offense and defense. It is important, however, that players understand that transition from offense to defense and vice versa is instantaneous.

Youth players often have momentary lapses when play changes from one team to the other. Naturally, this is a disadvantage to a team because it means, at the moment of transition, players are out of position.

While experience will improve this aspect of play, coaches can accelerate the learning process.

Most coaches work on either an offensive or defensive aspect of play in practice. This is quite normal. However, in their endeavor to emphasize the offensive or defensive principles, many quite often neglect counter-attacking or counter defending principles and objectives.

Therefore, I recommend that coaches in practice use a counter-attacking goal (objective). At the same time they should encourage their players to attack immediately they win the ball and to defend at the moment they lose the ball.

Realistic transition experience in practice will undoubtedly carry over into games.

Remember, the game is not offense **or** defense; it is **offense and defense**.

THE COACH AND THE METHODOLOGY

COACH

We have made the point in our other manuals in the *Coaching* series that **the game is the great teacher** and that the **coach** should regard himself as an "assistant"; an assistant to the game in teaching the players and an assistant to the players in developing their understanding of the game.

When observing and correcting players' roles in a game, the function of a coach is similar to that of a **car mechanic**.

THE MECHANIC:

- Looks at the engine

- Determines the part that requires attention

- Removes that part

- Repairs the part

- Replaces in the engine

THE COACH:

- Looks at the game

- Determines the aspect of the game which requires attention

- Works on that aspect of the game in isolation*

- Observes the performances of the players in the next game

Naturally, the coach does not have the luxury of a car mechanic who can replace a defective part. The youth coach must persevere with his players.

   * *This form of practice may be accomplished in several ways. The methods described in this manual are:*

- **A Conditioned Game**

- **A Functional Practice**

- **Attack vs Defense (Phase of Play Practice)**

METHOD

Conditioned Game

A conditioned game is a two-way game — with a goal and goalkeeper at each end of the playing area. Rules are imposed on the game by the coach to highlight particular aspects of play to ensure realistic practice. **Illustration 22** shows a conditioned game for sweepers; please see game rules on Page 49.

Functional Practice

A functional practice is designed to observe a function of a player or a small group of players in isolation. The game, played to a goal in one direction and a target in the opposite direction, is played in the exact area of the field that the player operates. Realistic numbers of players should be used for the size of the playing area. **Illustration 23** shows a functional practice for an overlapping player; please see game rules on Page 47.

Attack vs Defense

An Attack vs Defense practice is very similar in concept to a functional practice. However, instead of working on the function of one player or a small group, the objective of this practice is to develop team attacking or defensive understanding. Please see game rules for a defensive practice on Page 46.

Coaching Position

A coach should monitor the practice from "outside" the activity and not in the middle of the play. This gives him a much better "picture" of the game.

Illustration 22

Illustration 22 shows a **Conditioned Game** with the coach standing outside the touchline at the halfway line; this provides the best view of the game. Note the position of the coach in the **Functional Practice** and **Attack vs Defense** games (**Illustrations 23** and **24**) on the next page. His position in the non-playing area of the field allows him an excellent view of players' positions.

Related Coaching Points

- Outline briefly to the players, preferably by walk-through demonstration, the expectations of the practice.

- If practice is not succeeding and you are sure of the analysis, stop the practice and show what could have been done.

- Encourage and show briefly what was done well.

- Don't stop the practice too much or interest will diminish.

- Play the game no longer than 30 minutes.

- Keep the score to create a challenge.

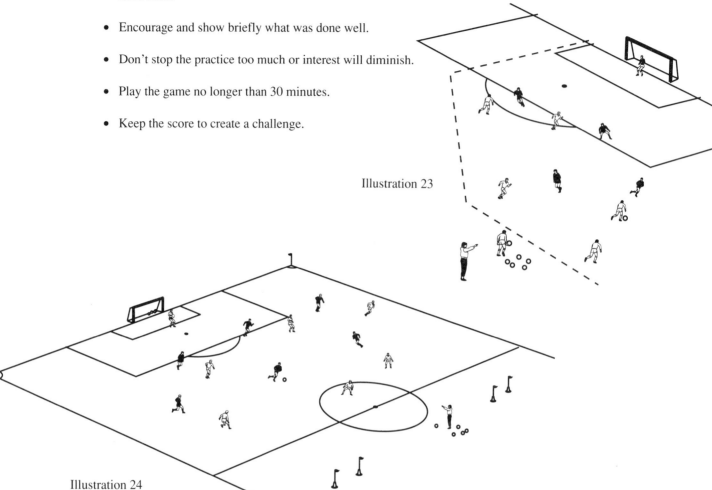

Illustration 23

Illustration 24

SIMPLICITY IS GENIUS

"The beauty of the game of soccer is in its simplicity."

Ron Greenwood, former manager of West Ham United in the 60s and 70s and of England in the early 1980s, not only believed in that statement, but also, impressed upon his young players to "Keep the game simple."

While he encouraged players to improve technically and tactically in practice, he believed emphatically that players should play to their strengths in games.

"Do the simple things well!" he would say, urging players not to complicate performance.

This is excellent advice for all young players who want to achieve good playing habits and become successful in the game. Soccer has a history of many thousands of young players who did not realize their ambition because they tried to complicate their game.

THE SOCCER SANDWICH

Many experienced coaches have found their own formula for conducting successful practices, indeed there are many ways to achieve success.

In our book *Coaching 9, 10 and 11 Year Olds* we recommend "The Soccer Sandwich" as a proven method of organization for that age group. Consider using a similar format for incorporating **Functional Practice** into your training program for players 12 years of age and older.

Introductory Activity

10-15 minutes — This is an ideal opportunity to incorporate a skill activity in the warm-up. Players may work with a ball each to practice dribbling, turning with the ball, control etc.; or in pairs or threes to practice various aspects of passing, control etc. There should be plenty of movement of the players and movement of the ball. Static stretches should be incorporated into the warm-up.

Game

20 minutes — Soccer players are all kids and kids like to play games. Play small-sided games to develop the technique highlighted in the warm-up. If passing and support were the themes of the warm-up (technique), use a small-sided game to highlight passing and support (tactics). Examples of games start on Page 57.

Functional Practice

25-30 minutes — Having identified the positional problem in the game, play a game from this book which will highlight the position.

Game

25 minutes — Develop the theme of the earlier small-sided game by using more numbers of players (e.g. 6 vs 6, 7 vs 7). While the larger numbers reduce the number of potential ball touches per player, players 12 years and older need to have the experience of cooperating in larger numbers to experience the type of challenges presented by the 11-a-side game.

The "bread and butter" of soccer is the **Game**. The "meat" of the training session is the **Functional Practice** in the middle.

If your team practices twice a week, I recommend this format for one of those practices. With change-overs from one practice activity to another, the above session will take as little as 80 minutes and no longer than 90 minutes. This is an ideal practice period for youth players.

THE PRACTICES

FUNCTIONAL TRAINING FOR FULLBACKS

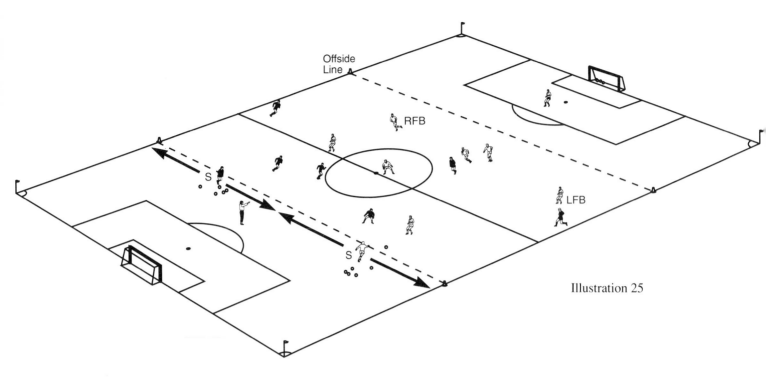

Illustration 25

Game Rules

- Set up the game in half a field plus 20 yards.
- The offense has three forwards and three midfield players.
- The defense has a goalkeeper, four defenders and three midfield players.
- The two servers must remain behind the line shown.
- One of the servers starts the game by playing the ball to the offense.
- Both servers act as "targets" for the defensive team.
- Throw-ins are taken when the ball goes over the touchline.
- When the ball goes over the goal line, play is restarted by one of the servers.
- When the goalkeeper makes a save he plays the ball to the defenders or tries to "find" the target players.
- Offense scores 5 points for a goal.
- Defense scores 1 point for an accurate pass to a target player.
- Forwards may be offside goal side of the offside line.
- Game duration: 20-30 minutes.

Player Objectives

Offense: To combine successfully to score goals.
Defense: To gain possession and play accurate passes to either target man.

Coaching Points

To observe the positions of the outside fullbacks and adjust when necessary.

FUNCTIONAL TRAINING FOR OVERLAP

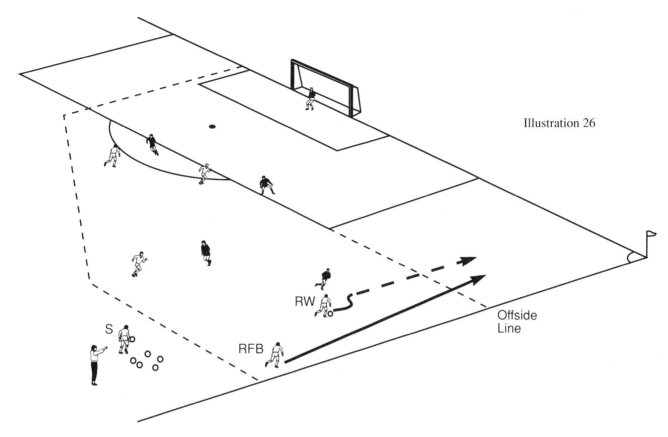

Illustration 26

Game Rules

- Set up game in the area shown: use cones or markers to create the area.
- Offense has one fullback, one midfield player and three forwards.
- Defense has a goalkeeper, three defenders and one midfield player.
- The server must remain behind the line.
- The server starts the game by playing the ball to the offensive team.
- **RFB** may have two touches only each time he is in possession of the ball **except** when he has made a successful overlap. After the overlap he has unlimited touches.
- Offense scores 2 points for a goal and 5 points for a goal from overlap.
- Defense scores 1 point for accurate pass to the server over the line.
- Goalkeeper throws the ball to the server each time he makes a save; his team does not receive a point for this.
- Server re-starts the game every time the ball goes out of play.
- The 18-yard line is the offside line.
- Game duration: 20-25 minutes.

Player Objectives

Offense: To combine successfully to score goals. To execute the overlap.
Defense: To gain possession and play accurate passes to the target man.

Coaching Points

To observe the quality of passes and timing of the runs to execute successful overlaps.

CONDITIONED GAME FOR MIDFIELD PLAYERS

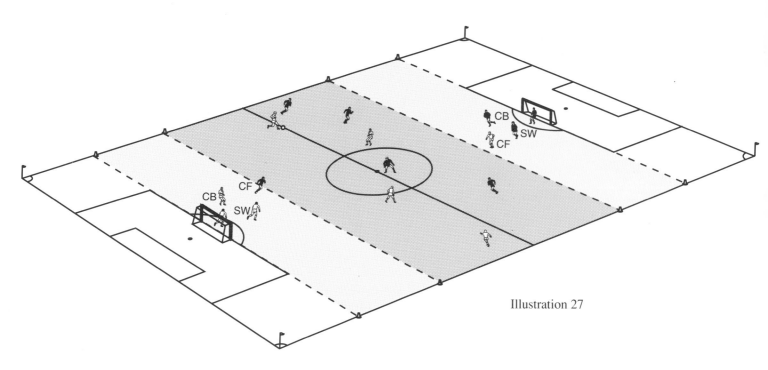

Illustration 27

Game Rules

- Set up a game between two penalty areas.
- Divide the field of play into three zones, as shown; the midfield zone is wider than the two end zones.
- Sixteen players are split into two equal teams. Each team has four midfield players, two defenders, one forward and one goalkeeper.
- All outfield players must remain within their own zones.
- Balls may be passed from one zone to another but not dribbled.
- The game starts with one of the goalkeepers who throws or kicks the ball into play. After a goal is scored the game is started in a similar way.
- The game has goal kicks and throw-ins but no corners.
- After fifteen minutes develop the game to allow midfield players to play in all three zones; defenders and forwards must remain within their own zones.
- Duration of game: 25-30 minutes.

Coaching Points

- Focus attention on the midfield players.
- Select one team of midfield players and work on the either offensive or defensive responsibilities of that team; do not work on both aspects of the play.
- Experienced coaches will be able to look at both teams and coach both offense and defense.
- This is not advisable for inexperienced coaches.
- Most coaches should look at **one team** and coach **one theme**.
- Please review the section on midfielders (Page 26).

CONDITIONED GAME FOR SWEEPERS

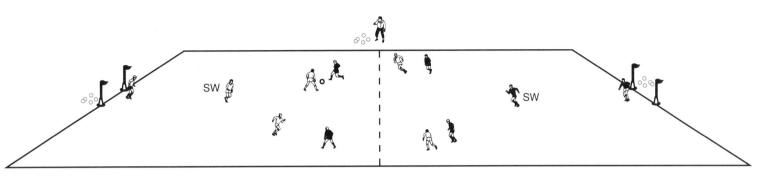

Illustration 28

Game Rules

- Set up the game in an area approximately 50 yards x 35 yards.
- Use 10 outfield players and two goalkeepers.
- Mark a halfway line with markers or place a cone on each touchline at the halfway mark.
- Three defenders against two forwards in each half of the field.
- Have a supply of balls behind each goal; one of the goalkeepers starts play by throwing the ball to his team.
- The forwards on both teams may not play in their defensive half of the field.
- One of the defenders may cross the halfway line only when the ball has been passed over the halfway line accurately to a teammate (forward) in the attacking half. Any of the defenders may cross the line but **only one**. Once possession is lost he must return to his own half immediately.
- Players may not dribble the ball across the line.
- Players may not pass the ball back from the attacking half to the defending half.
- Violations of the above will result in an indirect kick to the opposing team.
- The release of one defender across the line produces 3 vs 3 in one half of the field.
- When the attacking team loses possession, the defender must immediately retreat to his own half.

Coaching Points

Observe the functions of the sweeper(s).

In Defense:
- Communication.
- Covering position; how he supports his teammates.
- How quickly he steps up to deal with the third opponent in his half.
- How he defends in 1 vs 1 situations (see Page 16, outside fullback).
- How he adjusts to a marking position when a fellow defender crosses the halfway line to join in the attack.
- How he adjusts when the defender returns.
- How quickly he gets back from the attacking half when he has joined in the attack after his team loses possession. Assess his line of recovery towards his goal.

On Offense:
- Supporting positions when his teammates are in possession.
- Decisions — when and where to pass; accuracy of passing.
- When, where and how to join in the attack, and combination play with teammates.

FUNCTIONAL TRAINING FOR CENTER-BACKS

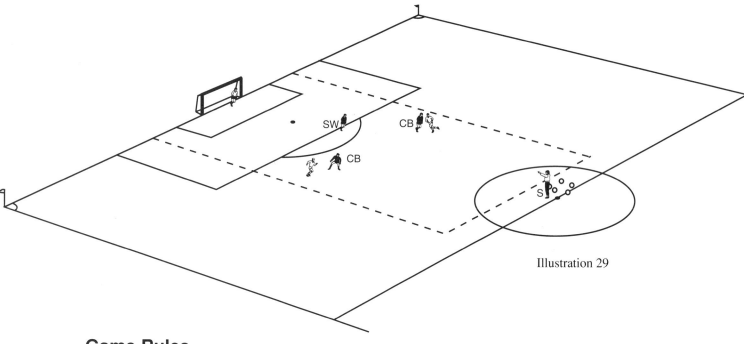

Illustration 29

Game Rules

- Set up the game in a channel, as shown.
- The defense has a goalkeeper, a sweeper and two center-backs. The offense has two forwards.
- The server remains behind the line shown, and starts the game by playing the ball to one of the front players.
- The front players combine to try to score.
- The objective for the defensive team is to win the ball and pass to the server, who re-starts the game.
- If the goalkeeper makes a save he may play the ball to his defenders or directly to the server.
- When the ball goes out of bounds, all play starts with the server.
- Offense scores 5 points for a goal; defense scores 1 point for an accurate pass to the server.
- Players may be offside only in penalty area.

Defense

- Communication.
- Starting position; marking position.
- How they defend as a small group.
- How they defend in 1 vs 1 situations.
- How they push up towards the server to deny opponents space in which to play.

- Game duration: 20-25 minutes.

Offense

- Supporting positions when teammates are in possession.
- Decisions — when and where to pass.
- Accuracy of passing.

Coaching Points

To observe the functions of the center-backs.

Note

- More pressure may be added to the defense by releasing a midfield player from behind the server's line after the ball has been played to the front players. This creates a 3 vs 3 game and requires more communication.
- Similar game may be played in a narrower channel where defense has a goalkeeper, a sweeper and one center-back.
- The game may also be played 2 vs 2 to force critical decisions and communication between the defenders.

FUNCTIONAL TRAINING FOR CENTER-FORWARDS

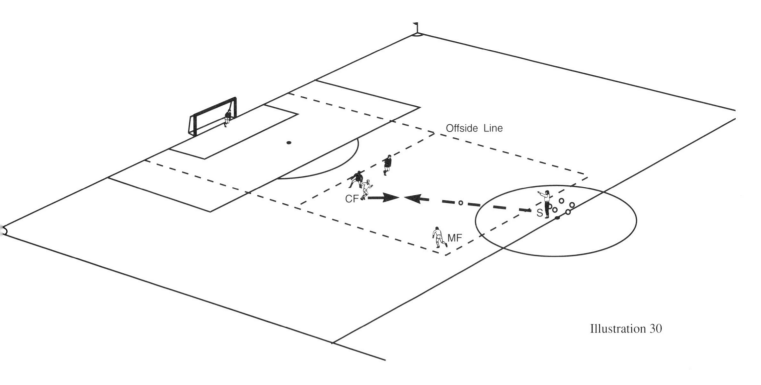

Offside Line

Illustration 30

Game Rules

- Set up the game in a channel, as shown. The defense has a goalkeeper, a sweeper and a center-back.
- The offense has a center-forward and a central midfield player.
- The server remains behind the line shown and starts the game by playing a ball to the center-forward.
- The center-forward may receive the ball in front or behind the defense.
- Once the center-forward has controlled the ball, the midfield player may be released to combine with the center-forward. This creates a 2 vs 2 game.
- The objective of the forwards is to score.
- The objective of the defensive team is to win the ball and pass to the server, who restarts the game.
- When the goalkeeper makes a save he plays the ball directly to the server.
- When the ball goes out of bounds, all play starts with the server.
- Have two defenders, another center-forward and midfield player waiting as alternates.
- Offense scores 5 points for a goal. Defense scores 1 point for an accurate pass to the server.
- Forwards may be offside goal side of the offside line.
- Game duration: 20-25 minutes.

Coaching Points

- To observe the functions of the center-forward.
- Movement to "lose" defender.
- Timing of his runs to receive ball.
- Control and shielding ability.
- Decisions — to turn with the ball in order to take on opponents or to lay the ball off to supporting player.
- Combination play with midfield player.
- Creation of shooting opportunities; accurate shooting.

Note

The game may be expanded by adding another striker and another defender. This creates a 3 vs 3 game.

FUNCTIONAL PLAY FOR WINGER & CENTER-FORWARDS

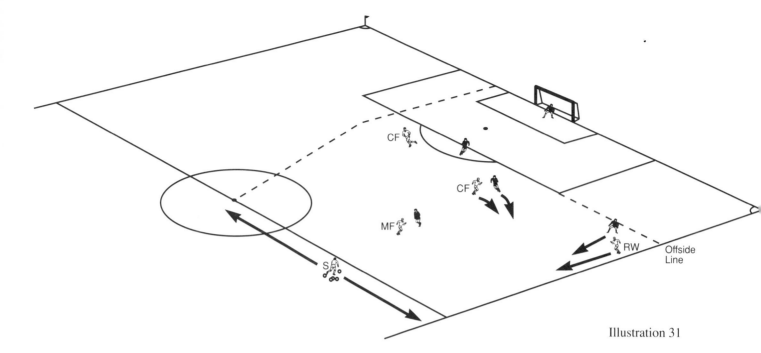

Illustration 31

Game Rules

- Set up game in the area shown. Use cones or markers to create the area.
- Offense has a right winger, two center-forwards and a midfield player.
- Defense has a goalkeeper, three defenders and a midfield player.
- The server must remain behind the halfway line and starts the game by playing the ball to right winger.
- Offense scores 5 points for a goal scored directly from a cross or 3 points for a goal in free play.
- Defense scores 1 point for an accurate pass to the server.
- Goalkeeper throws or kicks the ball to the server each time he makes a save.
- Server re-starts the game every time the ball goes out of bounds.
- The 18-yard line is the offside line.
- Game duration: 20-25 minutes.

Coaching Points

To observe the functions of the right winger and the center-forwards.

Right Winger

- How he makes space to receive the ball.
- Decisions — to turn and take on opponent, shield or pass the ball.
- Faking, deception, acceleration; moves to get opponent off balance or to take him on.
- Pace and accuracy of crossing.
- Shooting at the appropriate time.
- Combining with front players for wall passes.

Center-Forwards

- Where and how to support winger.
- Timing of runs to near and far post in the penalty area.
- Combination play.
- Quality of finishing.

Note

A sweeper may be added to give more depth on defense; an attacking fullback may be added for overlapping option.

GAME FOR DEFENDERS PLAYING OUT OF THE BACK

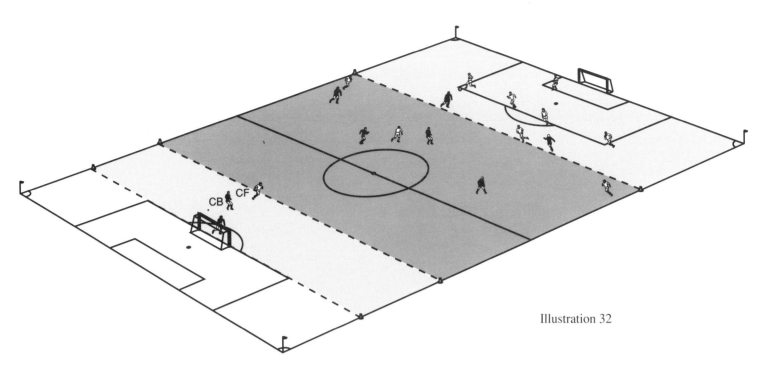

Illustration 32

Game Rules

- Set up the game in the area shown. One goal is set up on an 18-yard line.
- One goalkeeper, four defenders, four midfield players and one front player on the **white-shirted team**. This is the team playing out of the back.
- One goalkeeper, one defender, four midfield players and two forwards playing on the **black-shirted team**.
- The objective for both teams is to score in the opponents' goal.
- The **black-shirted team** is not allowed in the defensive zone when the white team has the ball; **CF** and **CB** are the only outfield players allowed in the attacking zone.
- The length of the midfield zone makes a pass from the defensive zone to the attacking zone unrealistic; therefore, the ball has to be played out of the back and into the midfield zone before it can be played into the attacking zone.
- Play starts with the goalkeeper in the defensive zone.
- There are goal kicks out of the defensive zone only. There are throw-ins but no corner kicks.
- At any other time the ball is "out of play," the game starts with the goalkeeper in the defensive zone.

Coaching Points

Observe the function of the **white-shirted team** only.

- Support for the player in possession.
- Mobility to create space.
- Pace and accuracy of passing.
- Compactness; how the team moves upfield as a unit keeping its shape and balance.

CONDITIONED GAME FOR ATTACKING SET PLAYS

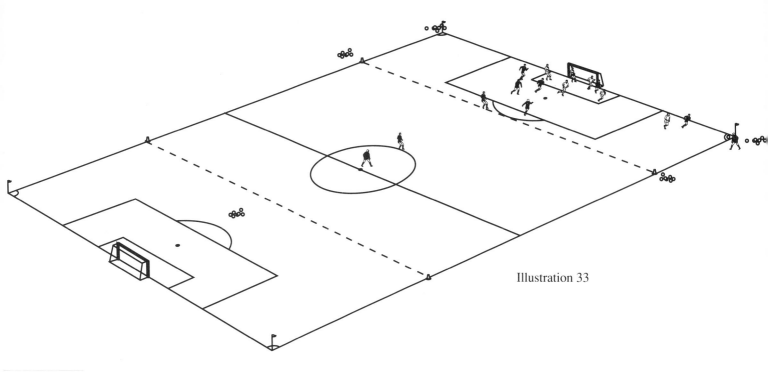

Illustration 33

Game Rules

- Set up the game in half a field plus 15 yards, as shown. Use cones or markers to make a line across the field 10 yards outside the penalty area in the playing area.
- Ten outfield players (the starting players for the next game) attack the goal in the attacking zone and play against the remaining players on the team. The starting goalkeeper can play in goal against the starting outfield players.
- Play starts with the sweeper just inside the non-playing area; the sweeper then becomes a "target" for the defending team.
- As the attacking team has more players they should be conditioned to a two-touch or a three-second possession rule.
- Each time the attacking team enters the attacking zone with comfortable possession they are awarded a free kick, corner kick or throw-in (designated by the coach).
- Three or four attempts at the set play should be practiced each time before continuing the game.
- There should be several balls around the attacking zone.
- The objective for the attacking team is to score from a set play.
- The objective for the defensive team is to play an accurate pass to the "target" player in the non-playing area.
- Duration of the game: 20-25 minutes.

Coaching Points

- Observe the functions of the players.
- Accurate execution of the set plays.

FUNCTIONAL PRACTICE FOR GOALKEEPER

Illustration 34

Game Rules

- Set up a half field practice as shown in the illustration.
- One goalkeeper and seven outfield players on defense; six players on offense.
- The server starts the play just in the non-playing half of the field.
- The object of the offense is to score a goal from a cross.
- The object of the defense is to prevent goals and to distribute the ball accurately to the server over halfway line.
- The defensive team is not allowed in the free zones on the flanks. This is to allow **X1** and **X2** to cross the ball. However **X1** and **X2** may be challenged if they dribble out of the free zone into the field of play.
- The offense scores five points for a goal; the defense scores one point with each successful pass to the server.
- When the goalkeeper makes a save he should pass the ball to his teammates or throw or kick the ball to the server.

Coaching Points

- Note position of goalkeeper. This changes with the movement of ball.
- Observe technique in dealing with the cross.
- Monitor communication between teammates and the goalkeeper.
- Analyze and correct distribution of the ball by the goalkeeper.

ADDITIONAL GAMES

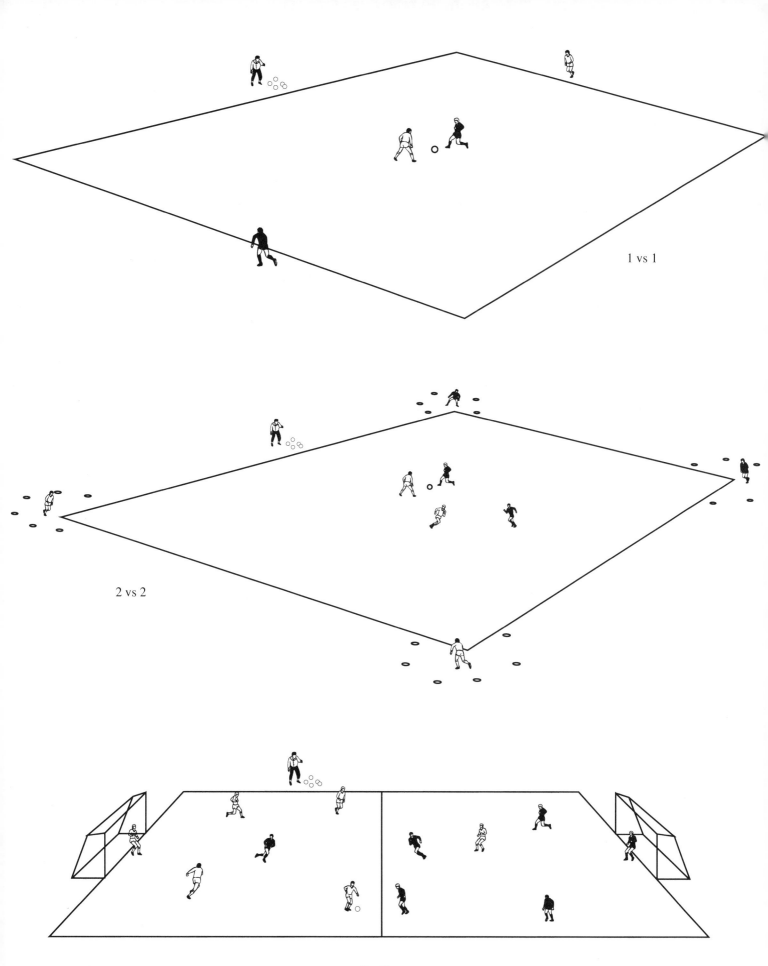

1 vs 1

2 vs 2

Big Shot

The Zone Game

The 4-Goal Game

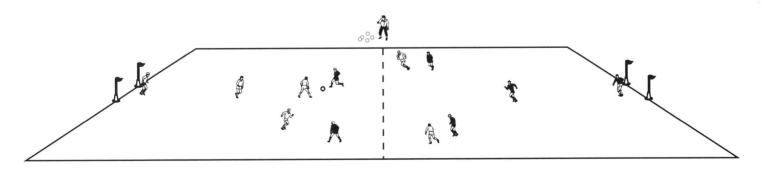

The Man-Marking Game

The **organization**, **game rules,** and **coaching points** for these six games are explained in detail in the manuals *Coaching 9, 10 & 11 Year Olds* and *Coaching The Team*.

APPENDIX

Thirds of the Field

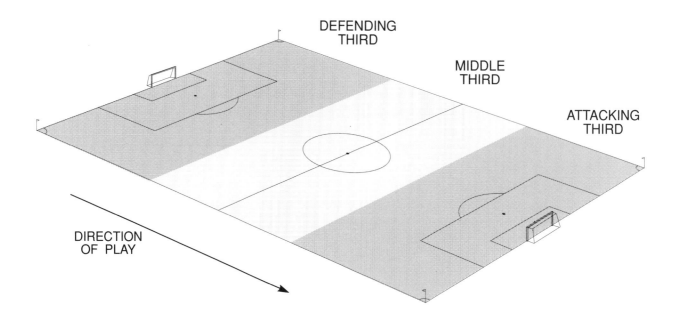

From a "strategy" perspective, it is helpful to think in terms of **thirds** of the field rather than **halves**. Certain things can occur in the Final or Attacking Third that would be irresponsible in the Back or Defending Third.

Attacking Third

The finishing zone of the field of play, where players should be encouraged (not criticized) when they take chances such as attempting to run and dribble past two or three defenders. Positive play here can pay big dividends and a mistake that causes loss of possession is not as critical as it would be at the other end.

Middle Third

The build-up zone. Ball possession is of paramount importance in this area. Great judgment is required in deciding whether to keep safe possession of the ball or play forward (penetration) to open up the defense — with the chance of setting up a scoring opportunity. Players frequently giving up possession in the Middle Third must be considered a poor risk in team terms.

Defending Third

The no-nonsense zone. Dribbling and back heel flicks by defenders may delight the crowd — and the opposing players — but not the rest of the team, nor the coach! "Safety first" has to be the maxim here — without resorting to panic play. Nevertheless, even though risks should not be taken, it is far better for the team if the ball can be brought out of the Defending Third in a controlled manner.

Offside

To the inexperienced soccer supporter, the **offside** rule is quite difficult to comprehend. Indeed, in the opinion of many, the rule should be abolished.

However, offside plays a very important role in modern soccer affecting shape, compactness and the balance of play. Also, space can be created both in front of and behind the opposition, stimulating the decision-making process for players.

The creation of space (offense) and the denial of space (defense) makes the modern game of soccer such an interesting game of strategy.

Players must be made aware of the strengths and limitations of the offside rule. For this reason coaches must incorporate the rule within the framework of their practices.

Bob Evans and Tony Waiters have written the book, *Teaching Offside*, to assist coaches and players to understand the rule.

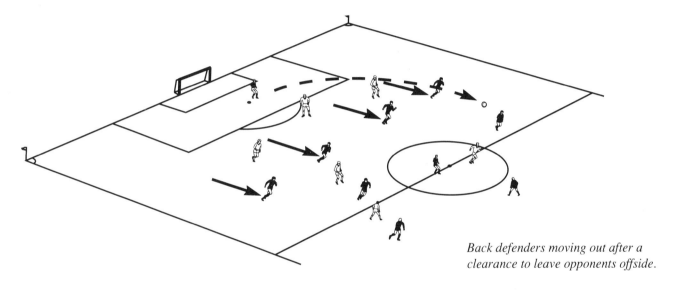

Back defenders moving out after a clearance to leave opponents offside.

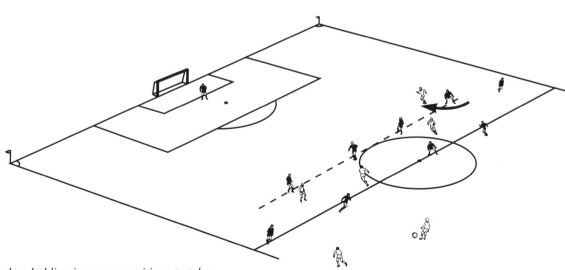

Back defenders holding in square positions to take advantage of offside. One can appreciate the risks involved with this tactic.

Glossary

AWARENESS: Cognizant of one's position on the field as that relates to the ball, teammates and opposition.

CHANNEL (n): Section of the field of play.

CHANNEL (v): Direct an opponent in possession of the ball into an area of the field.

COMPACTNESS: Appearance of a tight and firmly united team in the defensive mode; compactness is created by the distance between the front attacking player and the rear defender.

CONDITIONED GAME: Game with rules devised by the coach to highlight the topic being coached, e.g. two-touch only to encourage good supporting play.

CREATING SPACE: Moving to make room to receive the ball or moving to make room for teammates to receive the ball.

ENGINE ROOM: Midfield of the team.

FAR POST: Area in the vicinity of the goal post farthest away from the ball.

FIND (a player): Pass the ball accurately to a teammate.

FLICK-ON: Glancing header moving the ball off its original line but helping it on, generally in its originally intended direction.

FUNCTIONAL PRACTICE: Practice designed to observe the team role of a player or small groups of players in isolation.

GOAL SIDE: Closer than the opponent to the defending goal.

JOCKEYING: A delaying, "stalking" action used by a defender in a 1 vs 1 situation.

LAY OFF: Pass to a supporting player usually made by a player with his back to goal.

LOSE (an opponent) - OFFENSE: Move to "shake off" the close marking of an opponent.

LOSE (an opponent) - DEFENSE: Fail to stay with a mobile opponent.

MAN-TO-MAN MARKING: The responsibility of a defender to guard one opponent in most areas of the field.

NEAR POST: Area in the vicinity of the goal post nearest to the ball.

OVERLAP: Penetrating forward run "outside" a teammate who is in possession of the ball.

PHASE (of play): Half-field game or practice played towards one goal in an Attack vs Defense player arrangement.

PRINCIPLES: Established elements of the game of soccer which determine the nature and manner in which the game is played.

SCHEMER: Creative offensive player, usually a midfielder.

SELL ONESELF: Challenging too early for the ball, becoming unbalanced, or falling to the ground without winning the ball, giving an opponent an easy task in evading a challenge.

SHAPE: Outward form or construction of a team created by the distance between the front and rear players and the distance between the players operating on the right and left sides of the field.

SHIELDING: Protecting the ball by having the body between the ball and the opponent (the ball must be within playing distance).

SHOW (for the ball): Be in space and available to receive a pass.

STRONG SIDE: Ball side of the field.

SYSTEM: Numerical deployment of the outfield players on a team, e.g. 4-3-3 system employs 4 defenders, 3 midfielders, and 3 forwards.

THROUGH PASS (Through Ball): Well-timed penetrating pass.

TRACK: Run with and stay goal side of an opponent who is attempting to make a penetrating forward run.

VISION: Ability to "see" options in a game as play develops.

WALL PASS: Penetrating combination play involving two offensive players. Sometimes called a "Give and Go" or a "One-Two."

WEAK SIDE: Opposite side of the field to the ball.

WHAT IS ON: Options available for the player in possession of the ball.

WING PLAY: Attacking action on either the left side or the right side of the field.

ZONE MARKING: Responsibility of a defender or defenders to mark a particular area of the field and any player(s) who come into that area.